DEDICATION

To all of the villagers everywhere...

GRATITUDE

...and to all the days that help us up the mountain

And

The Story of More

Anna Elkins

wordbody

CONTENTS

Perhaps to hold on to the more,
we have to let go of the less.

&

AMPERSAND: A logogram representing the word *and*. The ampersand was originally a ligature of the two letters forming the Latin word for *and—et*. Over years and scrawls, the letters combined into the & symbol. When a *c* is added to the ampersand, it becomes the symbol for *et cetera:* "and so forth."

And so, forth!

ONE: THIS & THAT

Once upon a time, in a village at the base of a narrow river valley, the sun rose every single morning, even when people worried it wouldn't.

On clear days, it appeared for just a few hours in the space between the high, steep mountains. On cloudy days, it didn't appear at all.

The valley was a dark and cold place to live, but it was all the villagers knew.

Well, they also knew how to worry.

In fact, they were very, very good at it. They worried about whether *this* would happen and whether *that* would happen. They called it "what-iffing."

When they couldn't see the sun— which was almost all of the time— people would step out of their little gray houses, wring their hands, and shake their heads.

In the spring, they asked each other, "What if the sun doesn't come out and our turnips don't grow?"

In the summer, they asked, "What if the river dries up, and we have no water?"

Meanwhile, the sun kept coming up, the turnips kept growing, and the river kept flowing every single day.

In one of the little gray houses on the river, a girl named Day lived with her mother and father. Like the other children of the village, she grew up learning the art of what-iffing. But she seemed to do it all wrong.

When her mother sighed, "What if there is an avalanche?" Day would ask: "What if mountains could move?"

When her father huffed, "What if the river floods?" Day would ask, "Or what if the river brings a treasure?"

"How can mountains move?" asked Day's mother.

"Who would dump a treasure into the river?" asked her father.

Day thought about all the what-iffing over this and that. She wondered if *this* and *that* could possibly be anything more fun. Like different ways to eat a cookie.

Day kept trying to what-if like everybody else, but she had the distinct feeling there was something more.

This

That

TWO: DAY BEGINS

Day loved going to school. In stories and legends, she could glimpse a world far larger than the one she knew, even through her teacher's what-iffing.

Sometimes, it was hard to keep believing in that other world. Day's best friend Night would tell her it didn't exist. "What you see is what you get," he liked to say. Just like his mother said.

One cloudy afternoon during recess, after plenty of regular hand-wringing and head-shaking by both teachers and students, the sun burst through the clouds. The light was so bright that all the children in the schoolyard stopped playing hopscotch and started chasing their shadows.

Day looked up at the mountains. High above the edge of the valley crevice, the sun sent down a beam of light. It looked like a path leading from the peak to the village.

Quick as it came, the sun vanished. The children went back to hopscotch.

But Day stood still. She blinked.

Wait a minute, she thought. *The sun is right there—right behind the clouds. It isn't gone when we can't see it. So why do we what-if about it?*

She asked her friend Night, "Did you see that?"

"See what?" asked Night, keeping his eyes on the numbered squares chalked on the ground.

"The sun!" She lowered her voice to a whisper. "It's still there!"

"Oh, that thing," said Night. "Better not to count on it. My father says we could lose our turnip crop if it doesn't shine more." He shook his head in the exact same way his father did.

Day sighed.

All through the rest of her classes, she kept looking out the window to where the path had appeared on the mountainside.

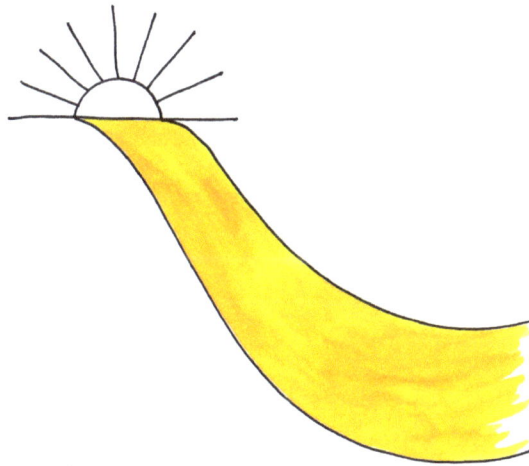

THREE: THE TREE

On her walk home from school, Day stopped and stood where the sunbeam had ended. A tree stood there. As she watched, its leaves began to shiver, and a bluebird flew from its branches and landed in front of her.

The bluebird cocked his head and looked at Day through one eye. "You saw it, didn't you?" he asked.

Day wasn't surprised that the bird could speak. She had always secretly wondered if animals could talk.

Still, she hesitated. "Saw what?"

The bluebird winked. "The path. You saw the path that looks like it ends here." The bluebird turned his other eye to look more closely at Day. "I'll tell you a secret. The path *starts* here. It *ends* up there." With his wing, he pointed to the crest of the tall mountain.

Day looked up. No one she knew had ever gone up the mountain. It was very steep. There were rumors of bandits in summer and avalanches in winter.

The bluebird was watching Day. In a low voice, he said: "The path appears to many people. But few do more than look at it."

"Why would I go to the top?" asked Day.

The bluebird tilted his head. "You must go to the top to see why you went."

Day looked up at the steepness. She looked back at the bird. She bit her lip.

The bluebird flew up to a tree branch. He asked, "What if you could see where the sun rises at one edge of the world and sets at the other? What if you could see where rivers start and where they end?"

Those were the first what-ifs Day had ever heard that sounded like her own what-ifs. The possibility in them seemed to open new doors and windows in Day's head. All sorts of thoughts started tumbling into her. There were big thoughts full of whys and hopes. There were also little thoughts about hows. But all Day could manage to say was: "I can't go alone. And I'd miss my best friend, Night!"

Day had an idea: "Can Night come too?"

The bluebird shook his wings. "For this journey, you must bring only yourself. If you choose to come, meet me here at first light tomorrow. Dream well."

And with that, he was gone.

FOUR: ALONGSIDE

At dinner that evening, Day thought more about the mountain than the turnips on her plate.

After dinner she tried to do her homework. Though she enjoyed her lessons, she wasn't sure why she had to learn so many rules. Her class had spent most of the day on language arts, and their teacher had assigned homework using parentheses.

"Mother?"

"Yes, dear."

"Why do I need to learn about parentheses?"

"Because your teacher told you to."

"But why did she tell me to?"

"Because her teacher's book told *her* to."

Day could see that this would end up nowhere. She set her elbows on the open book and looked at the definition again.

"Alongside" was the meaning of the two, curvy lines.

"Alongside," she said aloud.

Her father, reading the paper nearby, said, "What?"

Day closed the book. "Nothing, Father. Goodnight."

She climbed the stairs to her attic room and went to sleep.

That night, Day dreamt of an invisible friend. This friend walked alongside her wherever she went. As the two kept walking, the friend grew closer and closer, until Day could feel the friend's heart beat in time with her own. In fact, she wondered if it had become her own heart.

Day woke in the dark. She could feel her heart beating a strong, clear rhythm like a code. The minute she wondered what it was trying to say, she knew.

Yes, yes, yes, beat her heart.

Outside the window, birds were singing a dawn song. Day wondered if one of them was the bluebird.

She knew that *yes* was the answer to the bird's invitation.

She began to get dressed.

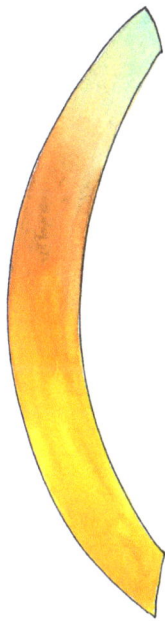 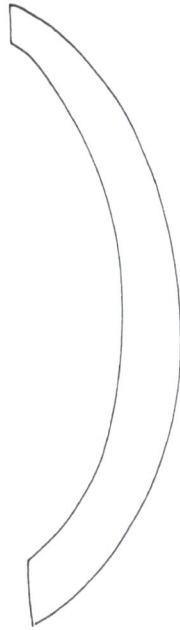

9

FIVE: HEART-SPEAK

It was still so dark that Day almost walked past the tree. The bluebird was waiting for her.

"Pssst!" she heard, followed by leaves shaking.

"I'm here," Day whispered.

"Come," said the bird.

"How long will it take?" asked Day.

The bird didn't answer. Instead, he led her up the precipitous path and asked another question: "Do you know why your village was built in this valley?"

Day shook her head. "No. My family has always lived here. All the way back to my great-great-great grandparents."

The bird asked, "What if you could live wherever you wanted?"

There it was again: another what-if that sounded like her own what-ifs. Day didn't know what to say, so she just climbed, trying not to stumble while the bird flew. To herself, she what-iffed how it would feel to have wings.

The bird continued, "What if I told you that once upon a time, your great-great-great-grandmothers and grand-fathers came to this valley to escape a terrible war and terrible things. When they found a safe place, they stayed.

They stayed until they forgot why they had come. And then their children stayed, too. But what you call home wasn't a place meant for staying."

"But we're all just fine there."

"Are you? Or have you all forgotten how to hear your hearts, just like you've forgotten that the sun always comes up, even when you can't see it?"

The valley was slowly beginning to open up as they climbed, and morning light was beginning to filter down the mountain. Day stopped to absorb the bird's story.

He landed on her shoulder. She reached up to touch him and felt his heartbeat.

Right then, she remembered her dream. Before she had a chance to tell the bird, he turned one eye to look at her and said, "You can do more than *hear* that heartbeat. You can know what it means."

"Like learning a language?"

"Yes. It's the better kind of language arts." He flew up and hovered above her. "Come on. We have a long way to go."

Day looked down. Somewhere below her, school would be starting. She looked up. Somewhere above her, a world with new lessons waited.

SIX: SOON

Day had to stop and catch her breath. It felt like they'd been climbing for hours.

She started to feel worried and… something else.

She called out to the bluebird, "I'm hungry!"

The bluebird circled down and landed on her shoulder. "For what?" he asked.

"What do you mean?"

"I mean: what are you hungry for?"

"Breakfast!" Day said, now hungry *and* annoyed. "What else would I be hungry for?"

The bird looked up at the still-distant peak. "Oh, many things."

Before Day could ask what the bird meant, a man appeared on the path.

Day stood very still, on the brink of a bad what-if. But the man began wringing his hands, and Day relaxed: she knew that gesture well.

The man said, "Excuse me, but is that the path back to the village?"

"Yes," said Day. "I've just come from there." As she said it, she felt a sense of accomplishment. She *had* just come from there!

The man nodded, "Thank you. I had heard that there was a land up above with plenty of sun. But I don't believe it. What if the story was a lie? Waste of my time. I'm going home."

Just moments ago, Day had wanted to go home, too. But as she heard the man what-iffing, she felt a new feeling: courage.

She heard herself saying, "Even if I don't see the sun, I think it's there. I remember one cloudy day I played outside. When I got home that night, I had a sunburn."

But the man wasn't listening. He just nodded absently and waved goodbye.

Day looked at the bird. "He was hungry for something else, wasn't he?"

The bluebird nodded his head. "Now you're getting closer, Day."

Day stopped. "Wait. I don't even know what to call you!"

The bluebird dipped his head in a bow. "I am Soon. At your service."

And then Soon continued leading the way up the path. Day followed, trying to remember if she had told him *her* name.

SEVEN: EVERLY

By noon, Day was truly tummy hungry. By afternoon, she simply sat down and refused to go on.

Soon alighted on her knee. "Why didn't you bring any food with you?"

"You didn't tell me to!"

"But you knew you were going on a journey. Why didn't you prepare for it?"

Tired and hungry, Day answered the question by starting to cry. Soon lifted his wings with an exhale. "Oh, stop. I'll show you where the berries are. Come."

Pouting, Day heaved herself from the ground and trudged after Soon. He led her off the wooded path to a massive bush of red berries. With a bow, he said: "Everberries for the hungry lady."

"Everberries?" Day asked, even as she filled her mouth with them. They burst like sweet jellies on her tongue.

"Yes. They always grow here, halfway up the mountain."

Everberry juice ran down Day's chin. "Are we already halfway there?"

Soon looked up. "Yes. Tomorrow you'll reach the top. The high places are surely worth the climb."

Day wasn't fully listening. She ate until her fingers were stained red.

"Come," said Soon. "It's getting dark."

Day had never spent the night anywhere but her attic room. She found herself what-iffing in the bad way: what if it was cold? What if there were bears or strangers?

She shook her head and let the unhappy what-ifs fall away as the sunlight faded. Day's legs were tired and her eyes heavy, but she plodded on, determined not to complain this time.

Just before dark, a small house appeared amid the thick trees. Warm, yellow light glowed through its windows.

"You can stay here," said Soon, as he flew to the door and tapped it with his beak.

An old woman opened the latch and smiled. "Day," said Soon, "This is Everly. She will take care of you. I must go, now. It has been a pleasure to walk with you. Good night."

"But..." Day started to say as Everly led her inside and sat her by the fire. Moments later, she brought Day a bowl of soup. Day accepted it with a smile and said, "Thank you. Do you live here alone?"

Everly sat across from her and watched the flames shimmy along the logs. "I am never alone. And neither are you." She looked at Day—not just at her, but into her. "When you have the infinite in your heart, you have far more than just yourself."

EIGHT: THE REMINDER

That night, Day dreamt the mountain path turned into a loop. She climbed to the distant peak and then descended back into the river valley—over and over and over.

Day woke up feeling strangely at peace. She walked into the kitchen, where Everly was already setting out two bowls of steaming porridge drizzled with honey.

"Good morning," said Day. "Is Soon joining us?" She licked honey from her spoon and reveled in its sweetness.

Everly looked out the window where bright sunlight shined in—the reverse of the firelight Day had seen shining out when she arrived by night.

Everly said, "Soon doesn't fly above the Everberries, and he must return to the valleys to show others their paths. But he will always be alongside you."

The sweetness seemed to dissolve from Day's tongue. She tasted a sour what-if and spoke it aloud: "What if everyone was right and it's a bad idea to climb the mountain?"

Everly crossed the room and took a small brown box from a high shelf. She brought the box to the table and opened it, pulling out a ribbon and handing it to Day. The ribbon was golden and blue—as if the fabric had been dipped in sunshine on one end and in the river on the other.

Day held it up, unable to tell where one color ended and the other began.

Everly said, "It is a reminder that you always have a choice."

"Between what?" Day asked.

Everly leaned close. Her face softened behind the steam of the porridge. "Between seeing things one way or seeing them another."

Everly finished her porridge and spread a blanket on the table. She placed wrapped parcels of food in the blanket, tied it up, and handed it to Day. "There won't be a shelter on the mountain, so you'll need all of this."

Day accepted the bundle, her heart and mind spinning. Everly walked her to the door and said, "We can choose to see more than what is visible. Sometimes the more comes easy like a river current. Sometimes it is harder, like a mountain path." Everly took the ribbon and tied it around Day's wrist. "This is a reminder to choose to see the more, no matter what."

Day looked at the blended colors. She what-iffed how it would feel to always what-if about the good. So she remembered the things she couldn't see: the dream of an invisible friend. And the heart-beat. And Soon.

As Day waved goodbye to Everly, she didn't just see a woman who lived alone. She saw so much more.

NINE: THE SPACE BETWEEN

By midmorning, Day had fallen in love with the sun. It made everything come alive with color and warmth.

Up and up, Day went, wondering why she had been what-iffing about the journey when the path was so easy to follow.

But just as she was thinking of stopping for lunch, she came to a split in the path. One way went to the left and one to the right. Neither went straight up.

Day had no idea which way to go. There were no signs. She could feel a bad what-if rising inside her. She wanted to pout, but she didn't.

She wiped the hair from her eyes. As she lowered her arm, she saw the ribbon. She remembered her choices. And then she understood: she saw that it wasn't so much a matter of choosing which path as it was about choosing how to respond to things on the path that could cause pouting in general and what-iffing in particular. That understanding was part of the more.

Day looked to her left and then to her right. She scratched her head and noticed the ribbon again: it was on her right hand, so she took the right path.

She walked and walked, and the path began to rise up and up. She walked through deep forests and across sloping alpine fields thick with flowers that tickled her legs. She walked up the path she was on until she'd forgotten there had been another one to choose from.

As the sunlight shifted and her shadow grew long, Day wondered if she was going fast enough to reach the top by dark. She could feel her heart beating a steady rhythm. It didn't seem to want to beat any faster, so she kept going at the same pace.

She was happily what-iffing about what she would see from the top when she reached a large stone. She climbed the path around it and found herself standing on the peak of the mountain.

But in fact, it was the top of just *one* of *hundreds* of mountains. Maybe thousands. Day set down her bundle and saw farther than she'd ever seen before.

Her first thought was that she could never climb all of those mountains. Her second thought was that she was thankful to be on *this* mountain at *this* minute. And her third thought was that she wanted to show the people of her village this most beautiful what-if she'd ever seen.

Of course, it was no longer a what-if. It was a what-is. Day lifted her arms and spun about in it, sending the ribbon of remembrance dancing.

TEN: AND SO, FORTH!

When Day returned to her village, her mother's hands were red from wringing and her father's neck was stiff from shaking back and forth. Her parents had been what-iffing the entire time Day had been away.

"What if you'd fallen and broken your leg?" wailed her mother.

"What if you'd been eaten by a bear?" huffed her father.

"But can't you see?" Day asked. "Can't you see that I didn't and I wasn't? And I saw the most beautiful places—places our great-great-great-grandmothers and grandfathers had seen. And I want to take you there, too. And...."

"*And* this, *and* that," grumbled her father.

"Exactly!" said Day. "*And* is even better than what-if! *And* is the *more* we don't see when we're what-iffing!"

Her parents *didn't* seem to see. But Day chose to stay hopeful, anyway.

At school, Day told Night about the mountain—about all the mountains.

Night mumbled, "But what if you had never come back? What if you had left me alone?"

Day poked him on the shoulder. "But I'm right here, silly! And we're never, ever alone, even when no one else is around."

Night's face brightened. "Would you take me up to see what you saw?"

"Yes, of course!" said Day. As she said it, the sun broke through the clouds and filled the schoolyard with light.

Day turned her face toward it. She asked Night, "What did you learn in class while I was away?"

Night smiled. "We learned about how the heart beats. I can tell you after school."

Day felt the *more* rising up in her heart. It felt like sunshine.

The weeks passed. Sometimes, the sun shone bright. When it didn't, Day reminded the villagers that it was still there, behind the clouds.

And so, in a village at the base of a narrow river valley, the sun rose every single morning, and people stopped worrying that it wouldn't.

In fact, they started wondering what it was like to live where the sun shone all day long. And when they were ready for the *more*, Day was happy to lead them up the path. One by one, the villagers climbed out of the valley, saw the vast, sunny lands high above, and chose to live where it was light enough to grow far more than turnips.

And after a while, they traded what-if for what-is.

And they lived happily, everly, after.

THE END
(& the Beginning)

EPILOGUE

This little book began with a vision. One morning, while having coffee as the sun rose, I saw a small line begin to rise up and curve around and around into the shape of an ampersand. I knew it was the shape of *more* and that it had a story to tell. So I returned to a tiny village on the Costa Brava in Spain, where I had spent many months watching the sun rise. I brought my traveling watercolor set and created the progression below, followed by the individual images in this book. That was the easy part.

But it took a couple of years and a long path to find the story that wove among the images. It was as if the ampersand's journey was illustrating itself in the journey of finding the words.

And then one day, the story came. Just like that. Just like finally seeing the mountainous horizon.

I knew that *And* wanted to be more than an idea in my head. And so it was.

And what-is.

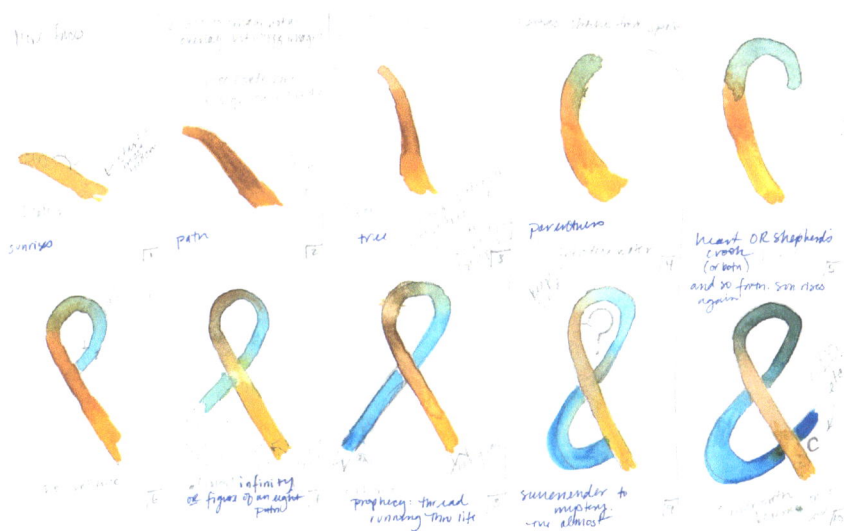

ABOUT THE AUTHOR

On her travels across the mountains and valleys of the world, Anna has encountered many marvelous people and heard their stories. She would love to hear your story of more.

annaelkins.com
ae@annaelkins.com

Other books by Anna:

The Space Between
The Honeylicker Angel
The Heart Takes Flight